Chinese New Year

Count and Celebrate!

Fredrick L. McKissack, Jr. and Lisa Beringer McKissack

Enslow Elementary

an imprint of

 Enslow Publishers, Inc.

40 Industrial Road
Box 398
Berkeley Heights, NJ 07922
USA

http://www.enslow.com

To Laura, David, Neal, and Allison.

Enslow Elementary, an imprint of Enslow Publishers, Inc.

Enslow Elementary® is a registered trademark of Enslow Publishers, Inc.

Copyright © 2009 by Enslow Publishers, Inc.

Library of Congress Cataloging-in-Publication Data

McKissack, Fredrick, Jr.
    Chinese New Year-count and celebrate! / Fredrick L. McKissack, Jr. and Lisa Beringer McKissack.
       p. cm. — (Holidays-count and celebrate!)
    Summary: "Kids count from one to ten as they learn about the history, symbols, and customs of Chinese New Year"—Provided by publisher.
    Includes bibliographical references and index.
    ISBN-13: 978-0-7660-3101-2
    1. Chinese New Year—Juvenile literature. 2. Counting—Juvenile literature. I. McKissack, Lisa Beringer. II. Title.
    GT4905.M44 2009
    394.261—dc22   2007046808

ISBN-10: 0-7660-3101-2

Printed in the United States of America

10 9 8 7 6 5 4 3 2 1

Illustration Credits: Associated Press, pp. 7, 15, 19, 28 (numbers 1, 5), 29 (number 7); Nigel Cattlin/Photo Researchers, Inc., pp. 17, 29 (number 6); Lawrence Migdale/Photo Researchers, Inc., pp. 25, 29 (number 10); © Ken Seet/Corbis, pp. 9, 29 (number 2); Shutterstock, pp. 2, 5, 11, 13, 21, 23, 27, 29 (numbers 3, 4), 29 (numbers 8, 9).

Cover Illustration: Shutterstock

Contents

Read About Chinese New Year!

Holidays bring family and friends together. People all over the world take part in different holidays. Chinese New Year is a lunar holiday. Lunar (LOO-ner) means the moon. Chinese New Year starts with the first new moon of the year.

lantern—A lantern is a special light. It is often made from wood and paper. It can be carried or hung up. Lanterns are a fun way to take part in the New Year. At the end of Chinese New Year, there is the Lantern Festival.

lunar holiday—A lunar holiday is a holiday that is set by the moon. Chinese New Year starts at the first new moon of the year. It begins between January 21 and February 20.

zodiac—The zodiac (ZOH-dee-ack) is a very old calendar. It starts over every twelve years. Each year is named after a different animal. People are thought to be like the animal named for the year they are born.

How many parades do you see?

One

In the United States, people take part in Chinese New Year with **one** big parade. The parade has many people. They dance, play music, and do special things. Acrobats, jugglers, and magicians perform tricks. There are marching bands and people on floats. They entertain the watching crowd. The sound of firecrackers can be heard, too. Some people take part in the Chinese lion and dragon dances. Parades in big cities are held at the end of the week, so people who work can come. The parade is a special time for people to come together in Chinese New Year.

How many oranges do you see?

Two

These **two** oranges have a special meaning. People believe that because oranges are round and golden in color, they will bring good luck in the New Year. They also believe that because oranges taste sweet, good things will come in the New Year. This might mean more money or good health. Other round and golden fruits such as tangerines and kumquats are eaten, too.

How many moon cakes do you see?
Three

These **three** moon cakes are small cakes eaten during Chinese New Year. They are so small they can fit into your hand. Moon cakes are always round. They have different shapes on the top. Moon cakes can be sweet or salty. They may be filled with sweet things like coconut. Some moon cakes have nuts and egg yolks inside them. Others are filled with meat. Moon cakes make people think of family, feel happy, and hope for money in the New Year.

How many legs does this lion have?
Four

During Chinese New Year, people do a lion dance. The lion dance is a dance for special times. Two people wear the lion costume. The lion has **four** legs and a big head. The dancers make catlike moves inside the lion costume. These moves make the lion look alive. The lion is thought to bring good luck and joy to people in the New Year.

How many red envelopes do you see?

Five

This man is handing out **five** red envelopes. People give one another presents during Chinese New Year. Children look forward to getting red envelopes filled with money. People believe that the red envelopes with money will bring good luck in the New Year. The red envelopes often have gold writing on them. The red envelopes are called *lai see* in Chinese.

How many petals are on this narcissus flower?
Six

The narcissus (nahr-SIS-uhs) flower is a Chinese New Year flower. It has **six** petals. It is special because it blooms in the winter. In China, narcissus flowers can be found in valleys. People often grow narcissus plants in their homes. Narcissus plants are thought to bring good luck and happiness. In the United States, they are called daffodils.

How many lanterns do you see?

Seven

At the end of Chinese New Year, there is a three-day festival. It is called the Lantern Festival. People hang lanterns on their homes or businesses. At night, candles or light bulbs are lit inside the lanterns to make them bright.

The lanterns come in many different shapes and sizes. The **seven** lanterns in this picture are in the shape of a pig. The pig is one of the animals on the Chinese zodiac (ZOH-dee-ack). The zodiac is a kind of calendar that changes every twelve years. There are twelve animals used on the zodiac. Each year is named for one of the twelve animals. In the Year of the Pig, people may use pig lanterns.

How many candies are in this tray?

Eight

There are **eight** candies in this eight-sided tray. Candies are eaten during Chinese New Year. They are thought to bring sweet things to life. Candies often taste like fruit. The tray is called the tray of togetherness. People believe that togetherness will help bring happiness, good health, and money to the family.

How many exploding fireworks do you see?
Nine

These **nine** exploding fireworks light up the night sky. Fireworks and firecrackers are used in some Chinese New Year celebrations. They are loud and bright. Firecrackers were first used to scare away bad luck. Today, some people still think firecrackers scare away bad luck. They also mean it is a joyful time of year.

How many people in this family celebrate Chinese New Year?

Ten

Family is very important in the New Year. People spend a lot of time getting ready for the holiday. They may spend days cleaning and cooking food. They buy presents for people in their family. Family members buy new clothing, too. They also get their hair cut before the start of the New Year.

The **ten** people in this picture are a family. They are sharing a New Year feast. During the New Year, they may visit other aunts and uncles or grandparents. They bring gifts for good luck in the New Year. Being together as a family is an important part of Chinese New Year.

More Information About Chinese New Year

Chinese New Year starts at a different time every year. It begins sometime between January 21 and February 20. The start of the holiday is tied to the first new moon of the year. Chinese New Year lasts for fifteen days. It is the most important holiday for Chinese people.

Chinese New Year is sometimes called the Spring Festival. The New Year holiday ends with the Lantern Festival. In China, people stop working during the New Year holiday. People in the United States often work during the holiday. Parades and meals are held at night and on the weekend so all people can take part.

People want to find good luck in the New Year. On the night before the holiday begins, people will light fireworks. People believe the fireworks will scare away bad things and bring good luck in the New Year. During the New Year holiday, people try to keep good luck from getting away. People will not use brooms, scissors, and knives because they do not want to sweep away or cut off good luck.

The seventh day of the New Year is important. In China, it is the day people celebrate their birthday for that year. People note their birthday by the year, not the day, they were born. Chinese Americans often celebrate the day they were born as well. Food is an important part of the holiday. Days before the start of the New Year, people make special food. Dumplings are one food. Dumplings are small boiled balls of dough with meat or vegetables inside. People often eat fish in the New Year. People believe eating fish will bring a family closer together. Lots of people visit family during the New Year. In the United States, people will with meet with other Chinese people if their family is far away.

Presents are an important part of most holidays. Children get gifts of money in red envelopes. Red is important during the New Year. People wear red. They paint the doors to their houses red. Red is a color that is supposed to scare away bad luck and bring good luck.

Count Again!

1		One
2		Two
3		Three
4		Four
5		Five

Count Again!

6		Six
7		Seven
8		Eight
9		Nine
10		Ten

Words to Know

acrobat (AH-crah-bat)—A person who can do tricks with his or her body like a cartwheel or a backflip.

dumpling (DUHMP-ling)—A piece of dough rolled around meat or vegetables and boiled.

kumquat (KUM-kwat)—A small fruit on a shrub. The rind can be eaten.

tangerine (TAN-gehr-een)—An reddish orange fruit that looks like a small orange.

tray of togetherness (TRAY OF tuh-GEH-thur-ness)—A special plate with eight sides.

Learn More

Books

Bledsoe, Karen E. *Chinese New Year Crafts*. Berkeley Heights, N.J.: Enslow Publishers, Inc., 2005.

Compestine, Ying Chang. *D Is for Dragon Dance*. New York: Holiday House, 2006.

Hughes, Monica. *My Chinese New Year*. Orlando, Fla.: Raintree, 2005.

Internet Addresses

Chinese New Year
<http://www.educ.uvic.ca/faculty/mroth/438/CHINA/chinese_new_year.html>

Crafts and Activities for Chinese New Year
<http://www.enchantedlearning.com/crafts/chinesenewyear/>

Index